WHAT PRICE DEFENSE?

*A Rational Debate
sponsored by the American Enterprise Institute
held at
American Enterprise Institute
Washington, D. C.*

PAUL DUKE
Moderator

WHAT PRICE DEFENSE?

Edmund S. Muskie
Bill Brock

RATIONAL DEBATE SERIES

American Enterprise Institute for Public Policy Research
Washington, D. C.

© Copyright 1974 by
American Enterprise Institute for Public Policy Research
1150 Seventeenth Street, N.W., Washington, D. C. 20036
All rights reserved under International and
Pan-American Copyright Conventions

Printed in United States of America

ISBN 0-8447-2053-4 (Paper)
ISBN 0-8447-2054-2 (Cloth)
Library of Congress Catalog Card Number 74-21550

FOREWORD

"To be prepared for war is one of the most effectual means of preserving peace." So admonished George Washington when the United States was in its infancy.

Today our country is a world power with vast responsibilities, and the price of preserving peace is high. Few doubt the wisdom of Washington's observation. But in this age of inflation, détente, and expensive weaponry, not a few are asking, "What Price Defense?"

Senators Muskie and Brock are articulate proponents of opposing views on this question. The cases they make during the course of this debate illuminate very well the difficulty of arriving at a consensus on this vital issue.

The American Enterprise Institute is pleased to present as the twenty-sixth of its continuing series of Rational Debates this contribution to intelligent discussion of a matter so important to the well-being of every American.

November 1974

> William J. Baroody
> *President*
> American Enterprise Institute
> for Public Policy Research

CONTENTS

I   FIRST LECTURE
    Edmund S. Muskie 3

II   SECOND LECTURE
    Bill Brock 19

III   REBUTTALS
    Edmund S. Muskie 41
    Bill Brock 43

IV   DISCUSSION 47

V   NOTES 73

FIRST LECTURE

EDMUND S. MUSKIE

Earlier this year, I spoke at the U.S. Naval Academy on the subject of our foreign policy. My thesis was that the United States is on the verge of a new coherence in its foreign policy, a new sense of direction and common purpose, and a restoration of the bipartisan tradition in America's foreign relations.

This restored bipartisanship, I argued, is based on a broad popular consensus on four fundamental principles of American foreign policy:

1. An isolationist policy is not a viable option for America.
2. The general direction of détente with the Soviet Union and China is an important American interest.
3. Our alliances with Europe and Japan are still vital, notwithstanding progress toward détente, and should be emphasized.
4. Our policies must reflect the growing interdependence between the developed and underdeveloped world.

A foreign policy based on these principles requires that America be strong militarily. I believe in a strong national defense. The issue in this debate is not whether America should be strong or weak—rather, it is whether the Congress can make any significant cuts in the administration's defense spending request for fiscal year 1975 without undermining our security interests or our foreign policy objectives. I am prepared to argue that it can.

FIRST LECTURE

The President's total budget request for fiscal year 1975 is $304.4 billion. Of that, $141.8 billion is controllable by Congress through the regular appropriations process. Of this portion of the budget which Congress can control, well over half goes to national defense. That is a sizable amount. Fiscal conservatives who have spoken eloquently on the tendency of government to overspend—and of modern bureaucracies to develop their own entrenched interests—should surely look with some skepticism at a defense budget of this magnitude.

Economists may disagree among themselves on how large the federal budget should be in a particular year—whether we should have a budgetary surplus or deficit, and how large the balance or shortfall should be. But within any given budget ceiling, we politicians cannot look to economists to tell us how to order our budgetary priorities. That is an obligation we have as representatives of the people, and how we make decisions on budgetary priorities affects not only our own political futures but, far more important, the future well-being of the entire nation.

It is the job of the President to propose a distribution of federal priorities, and it is the responsibility of the Congress actually to make the hard choices. The Congress, through the appropriations process, must decide how much to spend on defense; how much federal assistance to give to state and local governments; how much assistance should go to health, transportation, education, or environmental improvement.

Congress has the responsibility to make spending decisions which reflect the needs of the people. The nation's security is certainly a high-priority need, but there are others: federal funding for education is now only $7.5 billion; funding for drug abuse enforcement and prevention is only $750 million; for community development and housing, only $6.4 billion; for pollution control, only $700 million; for energy research, only $2.1 billion. Compare these figures to the administration's defense budget of $92.6 billion.

In ordering our budget priorities, the Congress must be prepared to trim back in one category in order to increase spending in another. My own view is that significant cuts can be made in the President's proposed defense budget for fiscal year 1975 which would free up several billion dollars of additional resources for helping to reduce the present tax burden, for reallocating to other areas of the federal budget, or possibly for both.

There is a pernicious view among those who habitually oppose cuts in defense spending reflected in the oft-heard slogan "Where national security is concerned, money is no object." This is a fine-sounding platitude, but the fact is that our total resources are always limited and must be allocated among many competing needs in our society. The nation has always compromised on national defense—even in wartime.

So tough budgetary choices must inevitably be made in defense, as in all areas of federal expenditure. While no President or Congress wishes to shortchange the defense effort, the unavoidable fact is that our society has other needs besides military power. Former Defense Secretary Robert McNamara expressed it well when he said some years ago: "I do not mean to suggest that we can measure national security in terms of dollars—you cannot price what is inherently priceless. But if we are to avoid talking in generalities, we must talk about dollars. For policy decisions must sooner or later be expressed in the form of budget decisions on where to spend and how much."[1]

The President's Defense Budget for Fiscal Year 1975

The Nixon administration has proposed to Congress the largest peacetime military budget in our history. The total request for the Department of Defense is $92.6 billion. To this figure, one can legitimately add the military budget within the Atomic Energy Commission (AEC)—for nuclear weapons programs and the like—which amounts to over $3 billion, and some additional funds used by other agencies for defense-related purposes. For purposes of this debate, however, I will use the Defense Department's own figure of $92.6 billion as the total request for fiscal year 1975.

This spending request is an increase of about $10 billion over last year's request: a $10 billion increase notwithstanding the fact that we have withdrawn from Vietnam—the costliest war in our history; notwithstanding the fact that we have an arms control agreement with the Soviet Union and that we have entered into a new era of negotiation; and notwithstanding the fact that the Nixon Doctrine calls for a much less interventionist foreign policy than we have had in the past.

Only recently President Nixon sent to the Congress a message, accompanying the report of his Council of Economic

Advisers, in which he said: "Too much government spending is the spark that most often sets off inflationary explosions. . . . We must work together to cut where we safely can. We must so discipline our present decisions that they do not commit us to excessive spending in the future." [2] What I propose is that we apply the President's tests to the defense budget.

Secretary Schlesinger testified before the Senate Armed Services Committee in February that this year's defense budget request in real terms "means doing no more than holding our own as compared to 1974." [3] The basis for this remark is that the difference between the fiscal year 1975 request of $92.6 billion and the fiscal year 1974 budget of $87.1 billion—an increase of $5.5 billion—is barely enough to cover pay and price increases. Technically, the Defense Department's figures are correct—except that there have been some dubious manipulations of the statistical data.

The figure used by the Defense Department as representing the fiscal year 1974 defense budget includes two items which really do not make sense for comparative purposes with respect to the fiscal year 1975 request. The first of these is last year's $2.2 billion emergency aid to Israel. This figure is not a direct part of U.S. defense costs, and the Defense Department has already announced that Israel will be expected to pay back $1.2 billion of this arms aid. As a one-shot aid effort, these funds should be subtracted from the fiscal year 1974 defense figure so as to provide a fairer comparison to the fiscal year 1975 request which includes no such amount for Israel.

The second statistical manipulation which serves to inflate the fiscal year 1974 budget is the retroactive inclusion of $2.1 billion contained in the supplemental appropriations request for purposes of buying new capability. Normally, supplementals are reserved for such things as emergencies or cost overruns. Out of the total supplemental request of $6.2 billion for defense, several billion dollars can legitimately be considered part of the fiscal year 1974 budget—including, for example, a $3.4 billion figure for pay increases. But $2.1 billion of the supplemental request is intended to increase inventory items such as ammunition and other supplies, increase airlift capability, accelerate production of the Trident submarine and, in Secretary Schlesinger's words, to "buy certain high-value weapons and equipment which are now in short supply in our Services." [4] These funds clearly represent an increase in real defense resources and should require a new authorization. This kind of request is normally submitted in the regular budget as a new proposal, rather than in a supplemental.

Despite the attempted distortion, the fiscal year 1975 request is still higher in absolute terms than any peacetime military budget in our history. The administration has attempted to create the impression that this increase results largely from military pay and the cost of the volunteer force. But compared to fiscal year 1974, other areas of the budget have been increased even more: procurement is up 23.4 percent; research, development, test, and evaluation is up 15.9 percent; and operation and maintenance is up 13.7 percent. By contrast, the costs for active duty military personnel have increased only 6.5 percent. If the volunteer force were terminated, no more than $750 million would be saved.

Where Cuts Can Be Made

The format of this debate will not permit a detailed analysis of the defense budget or a systematic presentation of budget alternatives. There are a number of public policy organizations which have done excellent work in this field—and their proposed cuts range as high as $15 billion. I believe that reductions amounting to at least $5 billion are not unreasonable—and certainly not unsafe.

Let me give some specific examples. First, in the area of manpower costs, which amount to over 55 percent of the total defense budget: the number of men in uniform has been dropping in recent years, in line with our withdrawal from Vietnam, the growing strength of our allies, and our new determination to avoid direct military involvement in regions which are not vital to American interests.

Still, far too many military personnel are involved in performing direct or indirect support tasks such as administration, logistics, training, or maintenance. Some of these support troops should be reduced.

Moreover, the U.S. should make significant reductions in the number of troops stationed abroad—bringing these men home and demobilizing them. The United States at present has 480,000 men in foreign countries—300,000 in Europe and 180,000 in the western Pacific and Asia. We have 36,000 men in Thailand, for no apparent purpose other than possible reinvolvement in Indochina. We have a full division in South Korea, twenty-four years after the outbreak of the Korean War, even though the South Korean Army already outnumbers the North Korean Army by two-to-one.

Our troops in Europe can be pared down as our allies assume a greater share of the burden for their own conventional defense. A 25 percent reduction in U.S. forces overseas would hardly signal an isolationist policy.

This year, the administration is asking for a further increase in the number of civilian positions in the Defense Department even though there are already over 1.1 million such employees—nearly one civilian for every two people in uniform. Excluding the Postal Service, the Department of Defense has roughly as many civilians as all other federal agencies combined.

The Senate Armed Services Committee has already recommended a 2 percent cut in military manpower and a 4 percent cut in the civilian bureaucracy this year. I would recommend additional manpower cuts beyond this, emphasizing reductions in support troops and civilian bureaucrats, saving our taxpayers well over $2 billion in payroll and attendant operation and maintenance costs.

Moreover, it is time that something be done about "grade creep" in the military. Surely it is not essential to our nation's security to have more field grade and flag officers to command a force of 2.2 million men today than we had in 1945 to command a force of 12.1 million. Nor is our security enhanced by having 400,000 more sergeants than there are privates in the army, navy and air force. The Marine Corps doesn't have this problem—it has twice as many second lieutenants as lieutenant colonels and 23,000 more privates than sergeants. If our armed services had the same grade structure today as they did in 1964, we would save about $700 million annually.

Second, in the area of conventional weapons systems for our general purpose forces: here, defense planners have gradually moved toward what is called a "Hi-Lo" mix—certain very expensive, maximum-capability weapons systems complemented by less expensive and less capable alternatives. I welcome the trend toward less expensive alternatives at the lower end of the mix. Past procurement trends have been too spendthrift, favoring new weapons systems equipped with all the most advanced technologies regardless of expense, even when gains in performance were marginal.

For example, new fighters like the F-14 cost fifteen to twenty times what the jets of the Korean War cost. Even taking inflation into account, a Korean War Sabrejet would cost about $690,000 today—which happens to be about the same price as the average total cost of the new Phoenix air-to-air missile being placed on the F-14 fighter. This tendency to goldplate new weapons systems out of proportion to real military necessity must be controlled.

Substantial savings—ranging from $1 to $4 billion—could be realized by stretching out procurement of more expensive weapons systems at the higher end of the mix and by emphasizing the lower end of the mix where possible. Examples of expensive weapons systems for which procurement should be stretched out include the SSN-688 nuclear attack submarine and the DD-963 destroyer. Systems which might be cancelled altogether include the Airborne Warning and Control System (AWACS), the navy's F-14 aircraft program and the Phoenix missile being developed for it, and the army's renewed proposal for the main battle tank (XM-1)—which the Congress wisely killed in 1971. Examples of weapons systems at the lower end of the mix which should be emphasized are the patrol frigate, the sea control ship, and the VFX "austere" carrier aircraft proposal.

While the Pentagon has made much of the alleged decline of our conventional forces since the mid-sixties, the truth is that our "peacetime" force for the seventies, though quantitatively somewhat smaller, is qualitatively far more powerful than in the mid-sixties. We maintain essentially the same number of tactical air wings. The navy has the same number of attack carriers and three times as many nuclear attack submarines. The small decrease in the number of ground divisions from nineteen and one-third to sixteen during the last ten years has reflected deactivation of forces remaining from the earlier Berlin build-up and abandonment of plans to fight two and one-half land wars simultaneously in Asia and Europe. Given this perspective, the cries of alarm about the alleged decline of our conventional power should be viewed with skepticism.

Third, I believe that cuts can be made in the budget for strategic weapons systems. I recognize that strategic forces account for only about 20 percent of the U.S. defense budget. But we are engaged in negotiations with the Soviet Union designed to stabilize and hopefully to achieve reductions in strategic nuclear weapons systems. We need not accelerate our own weapons development at this time on the theory that this would strengthen our position at the negotiating table.

I am not suggesting unilateral reductions in the strategic defense budget which might undermine an overall equality between ourselves and the Soviet Union. I support a limited

Trident submarine program—although the pace of its development should not be geared to producing bargaining chips in the SALT negotiations. I also support the navy's request for funds to develop a smaller submarine to succeed our present Polaris/Poseidon force. Our undersea deterrent is the backbone of our strategic nuclear forces.

But I have serious doubts about the directions being taken in our strategic bomber programs. The B-1 bomber is a typical example of a goldplated weapon system in financial difficulty. The unit cost of these planes has been rising steadily—now amounting to over $60 million per plane. I am concerned as to whether its ability to penetrate enemy airspace might be outpaced by advances in air defense technology before the aircraft is ready for deployment. My own preference would be for the air force to develop a less expensive stand-off bomber capable of firing its missiles from a position outside of enemy territory. Cancellation of the B-1 bomber program would save $500 million this year.

I also have serious questions about the administration's relatively modest request for development funds to improve the counterforce capabilities of our strategic missile forces. These funds are to implement Secretary Schlesinger's new strategy, involving improvements or changes in the targeting, the command and control, the accuracy, and the yield of U.S. strategic nuclear weapons. The military reason for this change is the assumed need to fill a perceived "gap" at the lower end of the spectrum of strategic nuclear deterrence. Along with this, there is the requirement, often mentioned by President Nixon, to multiply the options available to national leaders in the event deterrence fails. Both of these requirements can be satisfied, we are told, by the institution of greater flexibility in our targeting capability and in our hardware. With more rapid retargeting, with greater terminal accuracy, and with greater warhead yield, national leaders will obtain the ability to fight controlled or limited nuclear war by concentrating, if deterrence fails, on so-called military targets in a tit-for-tat fashion. This capacity, it is said, will also enhance the psychology or credibility of deterrence.

On the political side, a paradiplomatic function is claimed for the recommended changes in U.S. strategic forces. Their advent is expected to disabuse Soviet leaders of any notions that they may have that their new missile programs (the SS-X-16, SS-X-17, SS-X-18, and SS-X-19) will gain them a commanding lead in strategic weapons, assuming that this is their perception or motivation in this matter. If the Soviets see our willingness to commit our long lead in technology to the arms race, so the scenario runs, they will give up their own programs and negotiate more productively in the strategic arms limitation talks. Further, it is anticipated, this U.S. posture will reassure our friends and allies, convincing them that they can continue to rely on the American nuclear umbrella despite Soviet build-ups.

I feel certain that there are few, if any, members of Congress who doubt the desirability of improving our command and control systems and our retargeting capacity. What causes concern are improvements in accuracy and yield, especially simultaneous improvements in these areas. Here I would like to recall the previous and emphatic statements of this administration—both President Nixon and former

Secretary Laird—that the U.S. would resist any initiative that gave even "the appearance" of going for a first-strike or "silo-smashing" nuclear force, because it would be destabilizing and provocative. Accuracy and yield improvements, of course, give precisely this appearance. Thus, it is crucial that we know what now prompts this dramatic reversal in national policy.

A question also arises as to what price the U.S. will have to pay to get the increments of security which yield and terminal accuracy improvements are said to give us. What are the system-life costs of these programs? Can we be sure that we are really getting a greater degree of safety and security for our money? Or are we in fact buying programs which will increase the risk of nuclear war rather than diminish it?

The initial cost of following Secretary Schlesinger's recommendations for providing such options—new warheads, new guidance systems, and advanced work on a new ICBM—is not large in relation to other defense costs. The Senate Armed Services Committee has approved $77 million for research and development in three programs: $32 million for accuracy improvements of the Minuteman; $25 million to increase the yield of Minuteman warheads; and $20 million for MARV (maneuverable reentry vehicles). But these relatively modest funds could be the opening wedge for programs which in time could cost billions. I believe we should scrutinize this proposal carefully before appropriating these funds this year.

Finally, there is the administration's request for military assistance funds for foreign countries—amounting to nearly

$3 billion. I believe that at least $1 billion can be cut from that figure, with more than half coming out of the administration's $1.45 billion request for Vietnam. The American people have been led to believe that our involvement in Southeast Asia is at an end, and yet our continued assistance to South Vietnam, Cambodia, and Laos is extraordinary. It is time that we ask tough questions concerning the relationship between all military assistance and our real foreign policy objectives.

To summarize, I believe that some cuts can be safely made in these four areas of the administration's defense spending request for fiscal year 1975: manpower, conventional weapons, strategic weapons, and military assistance. Such reductions can be made, in my view, without jeopardizing our national security or our overall foreign policy objectives.

SECOND LECTURE

BILL BROCK

"What Price Defense?" is one of those classical questions that probably cannot be answered, at least to everyone's satisfaction. The problem is analogous, if not completely similar to another classical defense-related question, "What constitutes deterrence?" We have never *definitively* answered that question either; however, we do *definitely* know when "deterrence" ends, which is, of course, when war starts. In this day of nuclear weapons parity, "deterrence" has taken on even more significance because, as General Maxwell Taylor wrote in a recent article in *Foreign Affairs,* "strategic nuclear war must be deterred since it cannot be won."[1]

"What Price Defense?" presents a similar problem. How do we know "What Price Defense?" We do know that spending *too much* on defense at the expense of domestic priorities can cause a country to fall from within. We also know that *not* spending enough on defense can see a country fall in a more tragic way.

How do we answer this two-pronged question as to which issues should take priority in determining our defense budget, domestic priorities, or foreign threats and international necessities?

How do we know?—that is the problem. The problem is therefore epistemological, the study of knowing. I am not about to get into a debate on epistemology and whether cartesian, logical positivism, scientificism, or any of the other methods of *knowing* is best. However, I think that the only way we can even attempt *to know* in this type of subject is by the time-tested method of *comparison.*

Since we have a two-pronged problem of what should decide "What Price Defense?"—domestic priorities, or foreign threats and international necessities—we must try to answer our question by making a similar two-pronged comparison.

More specifically, we must:
1. compare our military position vis-à-vis possible foreign threats and international necessity, and also
2. compare the defense to the domestic portions of the budget.

Comparing Military Postures

To determine whether some $92 billion is too high, or even too low, we must look at what some of our potential adversaries are doing, and, unfortunately, I see some disturbing trends. Let me first turn to the other superpower in the world, the Soviet Union.

On the strategic level: first, we see that the Soviet Union is testing not just one, but four huge new strategic missile designs of various classes and characteristics. These are the SS-X-16, 17, 18 and 19. These new systems will incorporate improved launch, guidance, and reentry techniques, and at least three of these new missiles will be MIRVed (multiple independently-targetable reentry vehicles), adding a major new dimension to their offensive, their first strike, capability. We, meanwhile, have no immediate plans for developing new ICBMs and are still using the Minuteman missile which actually dates back to the 1950s.

Second, the rationale behind our letting the Soviet Union have a quantitative lead over us from SALT I (ICBMs: U.S. 1,054, U.S.S.R. 1,618; and SLBMs: U.S. 656, U.S.S.R. 740) was that we had a significant qualitative lead with our MIRVs. Now we learn that the Soviet Union is MIRVing at a more rapid rate than originally expected, and thus we might soon find ourselves with a qualitative equivalency and a quantitative deficiency which would be unacceptable. This could give the Soviet Union a possible first strike capability against our land-based missiles.

Third, we see that the Soviet Union has already deployed a new SLBM, the SS-N-8, on three new Delta-class submarines. These new missiles have a range of 4,200 nautical miles versus the approximately 3,000 mile range of our equivalent Polaris missiles. We, meanwhile, will not have equivalent SLBM missiles until our Tridents are launched five years hence.

Fourth, after letting their strategic air force capability lag for years, the Soviet Union is now deploying a new variable-geometry wing supersonic bomber, the Backfire. The exact role of this plane is still undetermined, although it will have intercontinental capabilities. We, meanwhile, are still arguing about the B-1.

On the conventional level: we see an even more disturbing trend. I am referring to the obvious change in the Soviets' naval strategy and their increased shipbuilding thrust. Until the 1967 Arab-Israeli War, it was conventional wisdom—and historical fact—that the Russian and then the Soviet navies had always been defense-oriented for reasons evident to anyone who has ever looked at a map of the Soviet Union. The Soviet Union is obviously a land power. Russia has never really needed a navy, even for their traditional, historical forays into such areas as the Balkans, Eastern Europe, Siberia, and India via Afghanistan. For the traditional, nationalistic thrusts of Russia, a navy simply was not needed.

Now, however, we see the Soviets building a definite offensive navy. Most disturbing in this respect are, of course, their new aircraft carriers and, depending upon V/STOL technology, which the Soviets are heavily pursuing, these could become attack carriers. The Soviets are also constructing a new class of guided missile light cruisers, the Kara class, which the chairman of the Joint Chiefs of Staff, Admiral Moorer, has described as "the most heavily armed class of ships in the world for its displacement."[2] The Kara class will be the first ship in any navy to be armed with three separate missile systems. And the Soviets still have, and will continue to have, the largest submarine fleet in the world.

The Soviet army has always been larger than ours, but recently they have made some improvements that could foretell a change in tactics. They have increased their troop levels in Eastern Europe from 390,000 to 460,000 troops, and most disturbing is the fact that they have improved their logistic capabilities, an area where we were always considered far superior. The recent disclosure that the Soviet Union was able, and willing, to move some major forces into the Middle East during the recent Arab-Israeli War leaves room for concern.

The Soviets are also continuing improvements in their air forces and have already started producing one new aircraft, the MiG-25, Foxbat, which is reported to be comparable to our new F-14s and F-15s which we are now just starting to produce.

Time does not permit me to give a detailed analysis of the People's Republic of China armed forces, but a few comments are in order. They do have the world's largest army and, of course, the largest manpower reserve pool in the world. On the strategic side, they have developed both medium and intermediate range (MRBM and IRBM) missile systems, and it is expected that by 1976 or 1977 they will deploy an ICBM system capable of reaching the United States. They are proceeding on research on solid fuel missiles, and have one Golf class submarine capable of carrying SLBMs which means that they could have an operational SLBM program within the next few years.

Frankly, I do not feel we can honestly consider the People's Republic of China as a major threat to this nation in the foreseeable future. Its greater potential for mischief lies in Asia and with the Soviet Union.

In sum, the question remains one of what defense is sufficient to deter the Soviet Union from war while we seek to encourage the movement toward true détente. I do not have a specific answer, nor does anyone else.

I do know our technological lead is rapidly diminishing, and further reductions in research and development can be made only at great risk.

I do know that Soviet investment in major new strategic weapons continues to climb and could result in a first strike capability within the decade.

I do know that Soviet manpower, firepower, and logistics capability is increasing in Europe.

I do know that our conventional forces are not only at a low level numerically but are inadequately equipped to defend themselves should that be necessary. And I do know that this circumstance can force us to reliance upon and early use of nuclear weaponry—an unacceptable choice.

I do know that the free world is more troubled than at any time in the past two decades. United States weakness, or the perception of weakness—whether real or not—could have a devastating effect.

In the face of these circumstances excessive defense cuts simply are not realistic.

Further, I do wonder how you can negotiate a reduction in arms with another power when you have already reduced your arms. What is there left to negotiate about, unless it is the hoped for comparable unilateral reduction on the other side's part?

When you couple this foreign threat assessment comparison with the next comparison, that of the defense versus the domestic budget, I would conclude that the defense budget is not an intolerable burden on the American people. On the other hand, neither may it be our most efficient expenditure, but more on that later.

Comparing the Defense to the Domestic Portion of the Budget

Nobody would contend that military spending is not high, and probably destined to rise even higher. There are three basic reasons for this:

1. Our increased personnel costs caused by the all-volunteer armed forces which both the administration and Congress supported.
2. The increased sophistication of weaponry and the need for this increased sophistication as witnessed by the recent Arab-Israeli War, and
3. Our now double-digit inflation with no immediate letup in sight for the foreseeable future.

Maintaining an effective military is, and will continue to be, expensive.

However, despite these more or less fixed factors, when you compare the defense budget to other economic indicators, there are some very encouraging signs. For the first time since the Korean War, the Department of Defense outlay as a percentage of gross national product (GNP) has fallen below 6 percent. The importance of this becomes most significant when we realize that even prior to our immersion in Vietnam during the 1950s and 1960s, the percent spent on defense was around 8, 9, and even 10 percent of GNP. In 1968, the peak of the Vietnam expenditures, the percentage was 9.4 percent and it is now 5.9 percent—a 3.5 percent drop in percentage of GNP, which, as you know, represents billions of dollars. According to 1975 estimates, 3.5 percent of GNP equals over $50 billion.

Comparisons to GNP are important, especially when you are trying to gauge the total effect of defense spending on the economy; but more relevant to this debate is defense spending as a percentage of the federal budget. Here, we see another very significant and relative decrease from past years.

During the 1950s and 1960s, the defense budget as a percent of federal budget outlays ranged from 60 percent, the Korean War peak, to the low and mid 40 percent range. At the 1968 Vietnam peak, the percentage was 42.5. In just seven years, this percentage has dropped to below 28 percent—an extremely significant drop of over 14 percent. According to current estimates, 14 percent of the budget equals over $42 billion. The 1975 defense percentage estimate is even lower, around 27.2 percent. In other words, the defense budget as a percentage of federal budget outlays has decreased from around the 50 percent which it used to be during the 1950s and 1960s to around 25 percent of the budget—almost a 50 percent decrease.

Why has there been such a significant reduction? The answer, as you well know, is not that defense spending has decreased in absolute dollars, but rather that domestic priority spending has increased significantly, as have our GNP and federal budget.

Since 1968, again, our Vietnam peak, the budget outlays for defense have risen 9 percent; however, all other programs have risen 121 percent, and the total U.S. budget has risen 70 percent. More specifically, human resources outlays have risen 173 percent, and this does not include veterans' programs. Being even more specific, federal budget outlays for education and manpower have risen 71 percent, for health 174 percent, and for income security a whopping 193 percent. It should also be mentioned that these are just *federal* figures and do not count what the states have provided since 1968, which would make these figures for domestic spending even more dramatic. Unlike funds for education, manpower, health, and income security, defense funds are solely dependent upon federal spending. For another comparison, our congressional legislative expenditures have gone up 161 percent, which does not compare very favorably to the 9 percent defense rise.

Returning to current dollars, there is no question that defense costs have risen. The total obligational authority (TOA) for the peak Vietnam year of 1968 was $75.6 billion while TOA for this year's budget is $92.6 billion. The rise is even more pronounced when you compare this $92.6 billion to the pre-Vietnam year of 1964, when TOA was only $50.6 billion. Therefore, in current dollars, we have seen an almost 85 percent increase since 1964.

However, in *constant* dollars, we get a very different picture. In fiscal year 1975 dollars, the costs are $92.6 billion for this coming year, $124.3 billion for 1968 and $95.4 billion for 1964. In short, in constant dollars, the defense budget has decreased slightly since 1964, the lowest pre-Vietnam War year, and has significantly decreased since 1968, the Vietnam peak.

Thus by three important measures:
1. as percentage of gross national product,
2. as percentage of federal budget outlays, and
3. in constant dollars,

we see that defense spending has decreased significantly, while, concurrently, spending for domestic priorities has increased even more significantly.

More specifically, we have seen since the 1968 Vietnam War peak:
1. a 3.5 percent drop in percentage of GNP representing some $50 billion,

2. a 14 percent drop in percentage of federal budget outlays representing some $42 billion, and
3. in constant dollars, a decrease of around $30 billion.

By any measure, we see significant decreases that also help explain that the so-called "peace dividend" was real.

In short, we might be arguing over nothing since the data seems to show that domestic priorities are already taking precedence in determining the size of the defense budget.

However, life is never easy, especially when you mix in politics and economics, and there is still a debate. Thus I would just like to say a few things about the argument over the defense budget.

This administration, this Department of Defense, like every administration and every Department of Defense, has always tried to put its best foot forward, which usually means trying to make the defense budget look as small as possible.

But critics, on the other hand, take just the opposite tactic to show increases and/or excesses. One favorite approach, and one used by the Project on Budget Priorities, is to compare administration *requests* for the current year to actual congressional *authorizations* of the previous year.[3] Using this technique, the increase always seems more significant. To compare properly, one should compare requests to requests or authorizations to authorizations.

Another favorite technique of critics is to add supplementaries to one year when they should have gone to another. And, adding to the confusion this year is a misunderstood remark by the secretary of defense that more money was put into the defense budget simply to "pump up" the economy. This remark, incidentally, has been denied by the secretary in a letter to the chairman of the House Armed Services Committee.

However, the important point, whether you use administration or critics' data is that there is a definite, discernible downward trend in defense spending vis-à-vis domestic spending.

This is the crucial point that I am trying to make in this comparison, and it is one that most critics do not dispute.

Now, this does not mean that 5.9 percent of GNP or 27.2 percent of the federal budget might not still be too high, especially when you realize that this comes to $92.6 billion. Therefore to see if this is justified, you must look at the other comparison: the comparison of the United States's defense needs versus possible foreign threats—a comparison that most critics fail to make.

After analyzing the preceding two comparisons, a case can be made for the adequacy of the level of current expenditures. The qualitative efficiency of this level could, however, be improved.

Four Principles of Efficiency

Although after looking at both comparisons, that of the defense versus domestic portions of the budget and then foreign threats, my conclusion is that the defense budget is not too high, since the cost demands of

1. increased personnel costs,
2. increased weaponry sophistication, and
3. inflation

indicate grave portents for the future.

I am very disturbed about these future cost trends, and believe that a whole new approach to our military budget may become necessary. I have in the past called for application of four principles of efficiency that I think will help us toward a realistic, yet effective military force at current spending levels.

These four principles are:
1. We should develop a staggered "phase-in" of new programs and phase-out of old ones.
2. I wholeheartedly support the so-called "Hi-Lo" mix where the highest quality and most expensive programs are supplemented by a parallel program of less expensive but adequate quality items.
3. We should proceed on a program of "capability without production" in some areas. This simply means proceeding with research and development but stopping short of costly production until strategic necessity impels further action.
4. We should develop a better "definition of roles" for the various tasks of our armed forces to eliminate duplication, and/or to adapt to changing conditions.

Time and space do not permit me to elaborate on these concepts fully, but just let me give you a few examples of each.

Phase-in. The central idea behind the staggered phase-in approach is that expensive new programs should not be begun at the same time as other expensive new programs. There are two reasons supporting phase-in:
1. Our economic resources may be unnecessarily strained

by concurrent development, and more efficiently husbanded by staggered development.
2. New systems phased in at the same time are likely to become obsolete at the same time, thereby necessitating a second round of budget-busting concurrent development, or worse, a need for combat use at a time when two important systems may be out of date.

Consider the Triad strategic concept, consisting of a manned bomber program, land-based missiles, and sea-launched missiles. Some question whether we need it at all, but I am not one of these. I think we do need the flexibility Triad affords us, but I think we need to devise a plan for proceeding one leg at a time.

In proposing a staggered Triad modernization, I recognize that I am saying that it may be necessary for our defense to be approaching obsolescence in one of three areas at any given time. But I believe we can reasonably set up a schedule whereby in the worst circumstances we will have superiority in one phase, parity in the second, and a possibly slight inferiority in the third. I view this as an acceptable strategic posture.

Phasing in the different legs of Triad is a good example of staggering development for more economic reasons. An example for phase-in for the second reason, to avoid concurrent obsolescence, would be if we had used this concept in developing our new fighter planes, the air force's F-15 and the navy's F-14. Had we phased them in, we would not only have avoided concurrent obsolescence, but perhaps they would have served as technical building blocks for new ideas and weapons systems.

Another example of phasing in for both economic and "dialectic" reasons could be in our close ground support systems. The Armed Services Committee has argued that we need both a fixed-wing aircraft, probably the new A-10 aircraft, and a rotary-winged aircraft, the army's new advanced attack helicopter, for close ground support. If so, they should be phased in.

There are many more examples of how we could save money by phasing in comparable or compatible programs.

Hi-Lo Mix. The Hi-Lo mix is a better known concept which I wholeheartedly support. I was extremely pleased to read recently that the secretary of defense has finally agreed to procure one of the new lightweight fighters under test, either the YF-16 or 17, as a "Lo" to the air force's new F-15.

The navy is deeply committed to the Hi-Lo mix and has many programs either under way or proposed to support this concept. For example, as a Lo to attack carriers, the navy is proposing sea control ships, essentially mini-carriers for escort and other duties not requiring attack capabilities. The navy also proposes to build about fifty patrol frigates, as a Lo for their more expensive DD-963 (destroyers) highs. The navy is also investigating the possibility of a lightweight fighter Lo to their F-14. And the navy is even investigating the possibility of building a new class SSBN, nuclear-powered missile submarine, the Narwhal, as a Lo for the Tridents.

In many respects, I hate to see these Lo's because they are definite trade-offs for better systems, and they also might give critics opportunity to ask why we cannot build an armed force of Lo's. However, because budget restraints necessitate them, I do support the Lo's of the Hi-Lo mix, but we should not be lulled into thinking that an armed force of only Lo's will be sufficient.

Capability without Production. Closely allied to the Hi-Lo approach is the concept of "capability without production." Our superiority at the highest level of technology is one of the most reassuring aspects of our defense posture vis-à-vis the rest of the world. We must never allow that valuable asset to be diminished for, as we look to the future, it is advancing technology that holds the key to military superiority and the preservation of peace.

Therefore, I strongly support research and development programs in wide areas of activity. I do not believe, however, that it follows that every good idea which is developed ought automatically to be turned into hardware.

There are many items whose existence in the development stage may be sufficient without committing additional billions of dollars to production unless the situation should require it. As the Brookings Institution stated in their *Setting National Priorities: The 1974 Budget,* referring to the SALT talks, "In the last analysis, the United States brings two advantages to these negotiations: its technical leadership and its superior economic resources."[4] We must maintain this leadership in technology and this might mean continued research and development without ever going into production. But remember that in overall costs, research and development are rarely more than 15 percent of final costs—a cheap price to pay for continued leadership.

SECOND LECTURE

Definition of Roles

In several areas, I fear that the roles of the various services, and of other operational aspects within the services, have become unclear. We need to sort these things out and establish some clear guidelines.

For example, we need a better definition of roles in our air missions. A glaring example of this is the fact that the Marine Corps is purchasing some ultra-sophisticated F-14s. It would appear that the Marine Corps needs these now to "fight their way into the beach," but when the Marine Corps has to start worrying about that, it has no business conducting an amphibious landing. Fighting to the beach is a navy function. What the Marine Corps needs is a good close support aircraft, perhaps the A-10 type.

With the all-volunteer armed forces and changing social and world conditions, we might find that the Coast Guard will have to take on some new roles. With the decline of the navy's vessels, the Coast Guard might have to guard our coast and assume escort duties for our merchant fleet. This will require the Coast Guard to reassess its role and for this reason I have recommended the creation of a new secretary of the Coast Guard.

We need new thinking about the role of manpower in the modern military situation. Our current forces are top-heavy with senior officers, the so-called "grade creep." The navy has approximately one admiral and ten captains for every ship, which is patently absurd. Similarly, staffs have grown out of proportion to real needs. Clearly, with the tremendous advance of communications, the need for large staffs has diminished. I was extremely pleased to see that the secretary of defense intends to add some more "teeth" at the expense of the "tail" of the so-called "teeth-to-tail" program by cutting staff support and using these cuts to form new combat battalions.

One need that has measurably advanced is the need for more highly educated technicians. For that reason, I would suggest the establishment of a set of military technical academies, similar to junior colleges, which would turn out highly trained noncommissioned officers who could make a real contribution to our defense needs. Similarly, changing technology calls for changing concepts with regard to the leadership roles for senior petty officers, another reason for increased training.

Finally, in the area of procurement policy, we need a new hard-headed look at our methods. I have introduced legislation to create a new Office of Procurement Policy within the Executive Office of the President in an effort to increase efficiency, clear away red tape and save money.

Conclusions

"Role definition" goes beyond just the military, and I would like to make two concluding points here, one close to my major legislative thrust and the second point which seems to me the real heart of this whole debate.

First, there is the whole question of the role of Congress in the budgetary process. Congress simply does not have the capability to look at the budget in any sophisticated way—we have no Office of Management and Budget. For over two years I have been fighting this problem, and early in 1973 I introduced S.40, the budget reform bill which has now come out of committee as S.1541. This will give Congress a specific role in the whole budget system which it should have. It will allow Congress to look at the totality of the budget and truly debate and determine national priorities. Obviously it is my contention that the maintenance of peace is a top priority, but under any circumstances Congress should play a major role in making such a judgment in the context of our total resources and needs.

My second point on "role definition" and the point on which I would like to conclude is this: the real question is not really "What Price Defense?" but rather "What is the role of the United States in the world?"

The question is not really what we should or should not spend on the B-1, the Trident, or even Diego Garcia, but what is the future role of the United States in this shrinking globe?

Should we retreat into isolationism as some seem to want? That could mean a very cheap defense budget, at least in the short run. All we would need are a few Polaris and Minuteman missiles. We could dismantle the army and cut most of the navy and air force. There are some that suggest such nonsense by trying to cut our conventional forces. They should realize that this would force us to early recourse to nuclear war in case of foreign threats. I, for one, would like more options.

Or, instead of sheet-over-the-head isolation, do we want a pluralistic world of freedom of movement, freedom of speech, and freedom of thought? If we do, it will require maintaining our present military strength in most areas.

I believe in and support détente, as I am sure every reasonable person does, but let us not be deluded by what this means. To Americans it means, as Henry Kissinger stated in January 1974: "Our view about détente is produced by the horrors that a nuclear war would inflict on mankind and therefore the obligation that is imposed on the leaders of all countries to do their utmost to prevent such a catastrophe from arising."[5]

All Americans would support this, but in the minds of many détente means that the basic underlying ideological questions between the United States and our allies, and the Soviet Union and the rest of the Communist world, between our capitalistic, democratic-libertarian way of life and their communistic way of life are being resolved—and this is simply not the case.

We see this very vividly in a recent *Pravda* article of April 2, 1974, entitled "Socialism and Creative Freedom": "The Western insistence on intellectual freedom is a cloak for subtle anti-Soviet propaganda. It follows from this that there can be no talk of ideological coexistence or even ideological armistice." "Creative freedom" that even denies "talk of ideological coexistence" is the best doublespeak example I have seen in some time.

I support détente, I support SALT talks, I support the Conference on Security and Cooperation in Europe (CSCE), and I support mutual and balanced force reduction (MBFR) talks, and I hope that they are all very successful; but let us not delude ourselves that major, meaningful, long-range changes are going to emerge from any of these talks as long as this very basic, but vitally important, ideological difference remains.

The "Role of the United States in the World" should be debated, but not in terms of specific line items in a defense budget. If we are going to cut funds for building a communications station at Diego Garcia, let us not cloak it in terms of "saving money," but rather face what it really means—increased hazard in the Indian Ocean.

For over a year, I have called for the creation of an informational, not legislative, ad hoc committee on national interest to probe into this question of what does the national interest now require in this era of détente, this era of increased material shortages, and this era of increased domestic demands.

Unfortunately, this call has not been heeded but, since nature abhors a vacuum, I am glad to see that our private "think tank" institutions like the American Enterprise Institute are sponsoring programs such as this so that we can publicly debate these vital questions.

"What Price Defense?" I really don't know, and don't think any honest man does. Let me just conclude then with a quote from General Maxwell Taylor:

> If indeed excesses have been committed in its name, that unhappy fact does not diminish one whit the very real need to protect those things which we consider indispensable to our survival, power or well-being, and hence deserving the expenditure of effort and resources to gain, retain or enjoy.[6]

REBUTTALS

EDMUND S. MUSKIE

I'd like to make several points. First, in my judgment, and I gather this is Senator Brock's, détente does not eliminate the need for a strong defense. Détente, as I view it, is simply a recognition by the nuclear superpowers that, unless they are willing to risk mutual destruction, they must find a way to reduce the possibilities of nuclear confrontation. That's all that détente is. So we need a strong defense.

Second, I don't buy the idea that any reduction in the defense budget represents a retreat into isolation. Senator Brock suggested that cuts in defense could be so interpreted by our friends and by our potential enemies. I would like to point out that there have been significant declines in defense budgets before: following the Korean War, for example. And the decline since the peak Vietnam War years, as a percentage of the federal budget or as a percentage of the gross national product, has not been as steep as it has been following previous wars.

Third, I don't think there is any reason for us to guarantee to the Department of Defense a fixed percentage of the gross national product, or a fixed percentage of our federal budget. There is no connection between measuring our defense needs and the size of the federal budget or the GNP. As the country's production and population grow, most domestic government programs must grow too. A larger economy with more people needs more schools, more roads, more social security payments, and even more tax collectors.

But growth in the economy and population do not, themselves, require proportionately additional defense spending in order to protect America's interests. I emphasize this point because the argument made by Senator Brock is often implied by our generals and admirals. They say, in effect, "You ought to guarantee us a certain fixed percentage of GNP." In my judgment, defense needs should be instead determined by an evaluation of our security needs and our long-range international interests.

I don't know how much additional time I have on my rebuttal, but I would like to make a fourth point, if I may. The argument is made that one of the reasons for the expanding defense budget is to meet the challenge of accelerated Soviet developments in the strategic arms field.

Let me give you just a few statistics which bear on this point. Since 1970, the United States has produced 758 additional missiles, compared to 492 by the Soviet Union; and 4,850 nuclear weapons, compared to 572 on the part of the Soviet Union. In the last four years, while our military people have been warning us about the development of Soviet strategic nuclear capability, they have tended to overlook the progress that we ourselves have been making.

I simply don't buy the notion that, because there has been forward movement in the development of the Soviet strategic nuclear capability, there must be additional increments of American effort on top of the effort we've already made in recent years to match it.

I think that these are issues that will probably emerge in the course of this debate as points of real difference between Senator Brock and me.

BILL BROCK

I'm not quite sure where to start, but let me take the last point first. I have no intention of suggesting that a percentage of gross national product, or the federal budget, should be allocated in perpetuity to the armed forces. I'm not so concerned about shares of the budget as I am about peace and the nation's security; and that's a more difficult area to judge.

I simply point out that since the end of the Vietnam War we have cut defense by more than $25 billion in constant dollars, whether you want to use 1968 or 1975 as a base.

We've also reduced its share—its strain on the economy—from 42 to 27 percent. We've cut its share of the gross national product from 9 percent to less than 6 percent.

Now, those are pretty healthy cuts. Let's go back to a pre-Vietnam year—to 1964. We've cut it from 8.3 percent down to 6 percent of the gross national product, 41 percent of the budget down to 27 percent. Any way you look at it, we have reduced defense spending significantly.

The question is not "What's the share?" but whether or not proposed cuts of the magnitude that the senator is talking about will, in fact, reduce our capability for defense, our capability for deterring an enemy. That's the question. Nothing else really matters very much to people whose children may be jeopardized, and that's the issue, I think, we've got to debate.

I cannot accept the mixing of apples and oranges, the measurement of very small U.S. missiles against the development of the SS-19, for example, which has a capability which we don't even approach in any program on the books, or even under any future projection I have ever seen.

It doesn't change the fact, and I will quote here the Brookings study, *Setting National Priorities:* "Taking everything into account, now there is probably rough overall strategic parity, but these—" and I will say parenthetically, these things don't happen overnight, and this is quoting, "Once the Soviets master the techniques necessary to obtain accuracies closer to those even now available to the United States, they would be likely soon to acquire a capacity to destroy virtually all the U.S. land based missiles in a first strike."[1] That to me constitutes a very real and present danger, and it is something that I find unacceptable.

DISCUSSION

DONALD LARRABEE, Griffin-Larrabee News Bureau: Both of you senators were deeply involved in the budget reform bill which passed the Senate this year, and during that debate there was considerable concern as to how Congress is going to get a handle on the overall budget. How can you get control over defense spending unless you enact some major reforms in the budget?

SENATOR MUSKIE: Well, this is one question on which Senator Brock and I have been, I think, in almost complete agreement in recent months.

The techniques in the bill for getting a handle on the budget are these: First, the bill would create a congressional office of the budget, which would give us the capability to get information, to analyze it, and to establish priorities. I think that's the key to any effective budget policy.

Secondly, it would give us the time to do an adequate job of budget analysis in connection with legislation. It would create a new fiscal year, beginning October 1st, rather than July 1st; it would require the President to begin making his budget submissions to the Congress earlier; and, in effect, it would allow the Congress about ten months for consideration of the budget, rather than the five we have now.

Thirdly, the bill would establish a timetable for the Congress to make the necessary budget decisions that lead up to the final appropriations bills at the end of September.

The last point I would make, and I hope I've left something for Senator Brock to cover in his analysis, is that the bill would force us, as a group, to focus on the unfolding picture of revenues and expenditures so that any votes we cast on the spending side will be made with full knowledge of what we can expect in terms of total revenues. If we vote to increase an appropriation for a given item, we will know, and the public will know that we know, that unless we want to be pictured as voting for a larger budget, we must offset that with reductions in spending on other items. It is a way of imposing self-discipline on the members of Congress.

I think these are some of the key points. I would appreciate having Senator Brock respond because, whatever our disagreements on defense spending, I think we agree that we need to improve budgetary control in Congress.

SENATOR BROCK: Now, I think that's a first-rate summary. We simply must have a structure within which we can debate expenditures in the context of our national priorities, whether you're talking about defense, education, welfare, or anything else.

I have a great pride of authorship in that bill. I introduced the first one two years ago, and I frankly never thought that Congress would ever impose that kind of discipline on itself, and I must add that I'm not sure it would have had it not been for the Senator from Maine, who is a great advocate. We spent a lot of time working out the details. I think we've got a good bill, and I think the people are going to benefit from it.

SANFORD GOTTLIEB, Deputy Director of SANE (Committee for a Sane Nuclear Policy): The question is for Senator Brock. The latest Defense Department annual report shows that the United States is about to have almost 8,000 nuclear warheads and the Soviet Union about 2,600 by mid-1974. That means we will have about thirty-six H-bombs for every major Soviet city. My question is, when do you think enough is enough?

SENATOR BROCK: I don't know that there is any definitive answer for that. I would point out two things. First of all, the Soviet MIRV capacity has just been refined, and it is now coming on line. That means that the balance is going to change markedly in the next five to ten years, which I consider to be years of great risk for this country.

Secondly, one of the things that we really ought to be debating tonight, and every other night, is what gets us into a position that might force the use of such a weapon?

One of the things that worries me most about the suggested cuts, proposed by some, for our conventional defense structure, is that you run, I think, the rather clear risk of forcing this nation to an early reliance on nuclear weapons. That's something I don't ever want to see happen. I'm not for an explosion in terms of numbers. We're not building any new Minuteman IIIs. We are refining our undersea weapons, but not so much in terms of quantity as we are in terms of quality and survivability, which is a pure deterrent; it is not designed for first-strike capability. We have never sought that in our undersea weapons, and I don't think we should.

The point is that if we limit our conventional capability we force this nation into a posture of reliance on the one weapon none of us want to use, and that's the thing I cannot accept.

AMROM KATZ, U.S. Arms Control and Disarmament Agency: This question is addressed to Senator Muskie, but I hope that Senator Brock will comment on it as well. I realize we're dealing with extremely hard and difficult questions here which are fraught with much uncertainty. No matter how definite the answers given, there is still a residual uncertainty. I don't really know how we know we're spending too much. I'm reminded, Senator Muskie, of Dayton, Ohio, which built five dams around it after World War I. That's like saying, "Let's get rid of the dams because we haven't had a flood since."

The question I have is, do unilateral cuts during the time of negotiations help or hinder negotiations with our adversary; and principally, do they help or hinder advancement toward the object of the exercise, which is international stability, peace and so forth?

SENATOR MUSKIE: I'd find it very discouraging if I had to believe that the only way to move toward arms control is to convert to its maximum the potential military power that each country has. And that's the logical extension of the bargaining chip argument. If one bargaining chip is an incentive for the other side to achieve a certain level of arms control, maybe two bargaining chips would persuade them to achieve another level, and three bargaining chips even more.

It seems to me that the United States has demonstrated an ability to build a strategic capacity which poses an unacceptable threat to the Soviet Union, and that it is in the light of that understanding, and of our understanding of their capacity to do likewise, that we've been moved to sit down together to negotiate meaningful arms agreements. I had this kind of discussion with Mr. Kosygin in Moscow two years ago.

We will not reach agreements of this kind unless we each see it as in our national interest to do so, and I simply do not believe that the amount of money we may happen to be spending on a particular weapon system in a particular fiscal year is going to be the final determinant as to whether or not we're going to negotiate an agreement. I just don't buy that kind of an argument.

Now, there is another point that I would make: as we build up our arms as bargaining chips, the other side doesn't really know whether our intention is simply to strengthen our bargaining position, or whether we have serious intentions of maintaining that kind of capability. I think they would have to assume that we seriously mean to maintain that kind of escalated capability, and that they must do likewise.

So it seems to me the incentive is in the other direction. I think the experience with MIRV is a clear example of this. During our MIRV tests, I urged that we suspend those tests so that there would be some chance to negotiate an agreement which would avoid moving into the MIRV era. But once we completed the MIRV tests, we inevitably moved toward deploying MIRV. Once we had done that, we knew that we had to let the Russians move into the MIRV era as well, and that's exactly where we are.

DISCUSSION

So our failure to exercise restraint with respect to MIRV testing and deployment resulted in an escalation of the arms race on the very eve of an agreement to enter the SALT talks.

SENATOR BROCK: The question is: is it wise, is it good policy, does it yield any productive dividend for us to engage in unilateral cuts when we're in the middle of negotiations?

Now that is something that you've got to answer in a very different way. Do we engage in unilateral cuts of our defense when we're engaged in negotiation in SALT II? If our objective at the SALT talks is to get the Russians to reduce their missile capability, then I think it's fair to assume that *their* objective is to get *us* to reduce *our* missile capability, *our* strategic arms.

If we're going to reduce our capability without going to the bargaining table, why go? The whole purpose of negotiation is to negotiate a balanced reduction. So unilateral cuts of a major consequence in the defense budget make negotiation fruitless and perhaps not even possible.

That's the basic question you must face. The fact is that the Soviet Union has never—not once in my entire life—unilaterally reduced its defense expenditures either as a result of our actions or something else, as far as I know.

They haven't demonstrated any willingness to cut defense. They have continued to increase their level of expenditures, their research and development, their capability, and they're getting a much too dangerous capability today for us to back off from bargaining as best we can, as strongly as we can.

SENATOR MUSKIE: May I respond further on that point? One, what we have in the 1975 fiscal year budget is the highest peacetime defense budget in the history of our country. So Senator Brock seems to be arguing that not only must you not cut any item of defense expenditure during negotiations, but you must increase defense spending.

If we follow that logic, our present defense expenditures should be at the highest level they reached in the Vietnam War, because any reduction from that level could be interpreted by this logic as reflecting a lack of will to maintain a balance with the other side.

This year the Defense Department has proposed, I believe, $146 million to improve accuracy and yield—in other words, to begin the development of a silo-killing capacity—for our strategic nuclear weapons. Now, there's an increase in the spending request. That's a bargaining chip kind of thing. If the Congress cuts something that's not yet in being—if the Congress says, "We don't agree, and we cut this from the budget"—should that option of the Congress be inhibited by the fact that we're involved in the SALT talks?

If you accept the logic of this argument, then I can see our defense budget rapidly escalating to $100 billion in order to maintain a bargaining position at the SALT talks. I just don't buy that.

ALTON FRYE, Council on Foreign Relations: I think that both senators have acknowledged that every defense budget has a vital diplomatic dimension as well as strategic and economic dimensions.

It's always difficult to judge how to threaten or coax an adversary or a potential adversary in diplomacy; yet we know that our own future defense budgets will be increased decisively by the behavior of the Soviet Union in its defense deployments. So it's very true to say that the negotiations under way will determine what price future defense will be for the American people.

In judging the specific negotiations in which we are now engaged and specifically the strategic issues that they pose, I wonder if both senators could give us their judgments as to whether we would be most likely to induce Soviet cooperation in restraining strategic weapons deployment by emphasizing to them that we will maintain the survivability of our own deterrent even if it means increasing our own force levels.

Or would we be better advised to try to induce them to cooperate by making clear that if they threaten our weapons systems, we will threaten theirs by developing a counterforce technology?

SENATOR BROCK: In other words, the choice is between survivability and counterforce?

MR. FRYE: Yes, sir.

SENATOR BROCK: I don't know that I'm qualified to answer that. I'm not sure that I can read that much into the Russian mind. I would like to be able to answer you, but I don't know. I have reservations about counterforce technology. I have very serious questions in my own mind as to whether or not that is something that is logical.

But the alternative to counterforce is called mutual assured destruction and the acronym is absolutely appropriate. I found it difficult to accept the fact that there is no alternative to mad self-destruction. And I would almost grasp for something that would lessen the possibility of war, but I don't know which, in this case, is the better alternative. To me, neither is a very good alternative. The far better alternative is to maintain sufficient strength now to force a negotiating posture on their part.

SENATOR MUSKIE: Well, I'll address myself to the problem of how we can maintain a credible negotiating posture that will not be taken as a sign of weakness.

You can get into all kinds of statistics, but I really doubt that year-to-year fluctuations in defense budgets are watched by the other side as a clue to what their next proposal at the negotiating table should be.

When I talked to Mr. Kosygin two years ago about this whole area of strategic arms, I didn't find him concerned about the then current debate on ABM systems in the United States. Nor did I find that his attitude toward the desirability of arms negotiations was particularly influenced by that debate. I'm not suggesting that he would have necessarily revealed his true attitude. But I just did not find it a lively item of concern on his part. So I don't really believe that year-to-year fluctuations, or disagreements between the Congress and the President over defense budgets, are controlling or determining factors.

I think both sides are mature enough to understand that the other side has a certain military potential which it can develop and deploy if necessary, that lead times are involved, and that we must be concerned with the long-term developments and attitudes of the other side rather than the year-to-year sparkle.

Consideration is now being given to the question of first-kill ability—in other words, counterforce ability, the ability to deprive the other side of the power to retaliate if attacked.

DISCUSSION

With respect to that, the Soviets have relied on fewer warheads with larger megatonnage, on the big bang—and it's that Soviet development that's regarded by some of our experts as a threat to our Minuteman missiles.

We chose to go for more warheads with a smaller nuclear bang. Our warheads are still pretty big, bigger than the bomb that knocked out Hiroshima. But we chose to go for smaller warheads, with greater accuracy.

Any comparison of the missiles of the two sides shows that we're accurate within .2 miles at best and one mile at worst (in the case of the Polaris A-2, which has the poorest performance)—but all our strategic warheads are accurate within one mile.

Soviet accuracy ranges from one mile to two miles. They simply haven't achieved the refinement in accuracy that we have.

Senator Brock mentions megatonnage—you know, the big Soviet bomb. They have an apparent edge in raw megatonnage of about two to one. But in terms of effective explosive power, not counting our forward base systems in Europe, we're about on a par.

I think Soviet attitudes are likely to be related to what they perceive to be our long-term attitudes and objectives as compared to what they know their own to be. They know that they can speed up development in particular areas if they want, and they know we can. And so I doubt that the dollar expenditure for a particular year is that much of an influence.

L. EDGAR PRINA, Copley News Service: I think the discussion is concentrated too much on the strategic arms area, which is a rather small part of the defense budget really.

I've often been struck by Congress's reaction to the defense budget. As soon as it arrives, everybody's talking about reducing it without having the benefit of looking at it. I wonder why nobody ever suggests that it might be increased. One should take a look at the other guy's spending and what he's doing in the arms business. Senator Muskie, you started off tonight by talking about how much Congress can reduce the defense budget and in your first ten minutes I don't believe you mentioned the Soviet armed forces.

I just wonder whether you think that there has been a failure on the part of the so-called anti-defense lobby, or the defense critics, to take up the discussion of what the Soviets are doing in more detail in order to give the American people an idea of what you're proposing.

SENATOR MUSKIE: With respect to the opening statement, the question that I was asked to answer was: can cuts be made in the U.S. defense budget? With respect to Soviet capabilities, I've already gone through what Senator Brock may think is a filibuster on those capabilities in answer to the previous question. I'd be glad to expand on it. The Soviet budget, I think, includes about $40 to $50 billion for defense. I don't know what that means, because I'm not enough of an economist to know what kind of values they get from expenditures in a controlled economy compared to what we get in a free economy. I have no way of comparing their $40 to $50 billion with our $90 billion.

MR. PRINA: Well, you can compare what they spend on manpower, though.

DISCUSSION

SENATOR MUSKIE: Yes. But I also understand that the Soviet Union is a land power with a hostile China on one flank and with Europe and NATO on the other flank, and that gives them a much greater requirement for manpower than we have.

MR. PRINA: I'm not talking about the numbers. I'm talking about the expenditures for manpower. As you pointed out, 55 percent of our budget goes for manpower and I think the figure is about 25 percent for the Soviet Union.

SENATOR MUSKIE: So they pay less.

MR. PRINA: Aren't they able to buy a lot more arms? That's what my point is. Aren't they spending much more on arms than we are?

SENATOR BROCK: First of all, I don't know how you can relate the two dollar figures because they pay a different price. They control their price, from men, material and everything else. You can say factually they have 3 million men under arms, which costs $18 billion.

We have 2.1 million which costs $44 billion. So we're paying much more for manpower. In terms of strategic investment, 9 percent of our budget is going to strategic forces now. That's awfully low—dangerously low in my opinion. Look at the Russian investment in R & D alone. Now, the senator was talking about our missile capability. I will accept at least for the moment the comparability of existent forces.

But I will not accept the statement that that condition will apply one year from now, much less five or ten with the SS-16, 17, 18 and 19, MIRVed and in place, if they decide to deploy them. Those missiles are virtually tested now and ready to go.

They've increased their troops in Eastern Europe in the last five years from 390,000 to 460,000 troops. They have 8,000 tanks.

They have markedly improved their logistic capability in the Eastern European theater. There just is no way you can compare the effort that we're making with what they're doing, either in terms of magnitude of investment, or in terms of gross national product.

They've developed their Foxbat—it's equivalent to our F-14 and F-15, which we are just beginning to produce.

They are doing a better job by far. If they are ready to go ahead with détente, they certainly haven't given us any indication of it.

FRANK VAN DER LINDEN, *Nashville Banner*: Senator Muskie, you know that while we are at peace at the moment, we have a very dangerous situation in the Middle East and there was a hot war there just a few months ago. We had to airlift large supplies of tanks and anti-tank weapons, ammunition, and other supplies to Israel to keep it from being overcome by the Arab forces.

I'd like to ask you, Senator, in case the war should resume in the Middle East, and Israel should again ask us to send over our most modern tanks and the anti-tank missiles, would you favor sending them everything they needed?

SENATOR MUSKIE: I don't think it's helpful to answer a question like that in terms of the situation in the Middle East. Coming from a United States senator, that takes the form of an ultimatum.

MR. VAN DER LINDEN: Aren't we pledged to protect Israel?

SENATOR MUSKIE: And that stands, but now you want me to address a hypothetical situation in which both Syria and Egypt, which have signed a withdrawal agreement, fail to observe the agreement. You assume a breach of the agreement by Israel or the Arab nations, or both, and then you ask me to anticipate what my reaction would be. I think that would be highly provocative.

MR. VAN DER LINDEN: Sir, don't you believe that our military must be prepared for just that kind of eventuality?

SENATOR MUSKIE: That's a different kind of question. Of course, I believe we should be prepared. But you asked me to specify what kind of aid I'd be prepared to send. And I just don't believe it would be helpful for me to speculate on that or to engage in a certain kind of saber rattling.

MR. VAN DER LINDEN: But every contingency plan is based upon something that may or may not occur. The question, sir, is would you send our tanks to Israel if they needed them?

SENATOR MUSKIE: We are pledged to provide Israel with the arms necessary to maintain a military balance in the Middle East. I consider that pledge still binding and I'm sure that that's a responsible way to answer the question.

MR. VAN DER LINDEN: I would like to pursue this question: where would we get these tanks?

SENATOR MUSKIE: We have an item in the budget for tanks.

MR. VAN DER LINDEN: Sir, how many tanks do we produce a year in the United States?

DISCUSSION

SENATOR MUSKIE: I couldn't give you that figure.

MR. VAN DER LINDEN: You should know, sir. The House Armed Services Committee reported last week that our total production of tanks for the entire United States for the entire year is 360 tanks, an amount which could easily have been destroyed in about one hour's warfare in the Middle East in October.

SENATOR MUSKIE: Well, I take it that what you're arguing by implication is that we should raise our tank production every year—that it should be geared to the capacity of the Middle East countries to consume them in a repetition of the war of last fall. I don't buy that conclusion.

PETER KROGH, School of Foreign Service, Georgetown University: Up until now, we have been talking pretty much in bipolar terms about defense expenditures. Without forcing you into instant research, I would like to know what has been the trend of defense expenditures among our allies and the extent to which you feel our defense budget should take theirs into account.

SENATOR MUSKIE: Well, our European allies, I think, spend between 3 and 4 percent of their gross national product on defense. We spend about 6 percent, I think, if my figures are correct. I forget what the Russian figure is. And so the Europeans spend less than we do as a percentage of their GNP, and we have undertaken to persuade them for some time that they've got to increase their commitment to their own defense so as to reduce the burden on us. I think that's a legitimate objective, and I support it heartily.

And there has been some movement. It could be better, and I think that's a major objective of the secretary of defense at the moment. As a matter of fact, I think he's leaving for Europe this week to continue his effort to get their expenditures up, to reduce the burden on us. And I heartily concur in that.

RUTH CLUSEN, League of Women Voters: I would address my question to Senator Brock. It seems to me that we've been focusing on the negative factors which influence the building of a national defense budget. So essentially, Senator, I'd like to ask you where in the proposed defense budget are reflected the favorable things which have happened during the past couple of years? For instance, the cessation of fighting in Vietnam, the improved relations with China, the increased trade with the U.S.S.R., and—at least for the time being—the successful negotiations in the Middle East. The American public, I think, feels it has a right to expect to see these things affect the national defense budget. To what extent are they reflected in the proposal?

SENATOR BROCK: Extensively. We have cut, in constant or real dollars, some $25 billion out of the defense budget. It would be that much higher today were we maintaining the Vietnam level. More to the point, we are reducing not only the constant dollar, but we are also reducing the load on the American people in very specific terms.

I might point out to you that there is another peace dividend that I supported, and I still do, and that's called a volunteer army. But you and I as citizens have to pay for this dividend. The volunteer army has been enormously expensive: about $20 or $21 billion over what we would have paid if we had maintained the draft. This puts a burden not only on our defense budget; it also tips the ratio of spending over to personnel from research and development, technology, and perhaps eventually even hardware. This makes it far more difficult for us to maintain an adequate strategic defense while maintaining a stable budget.

Yet we have been able to do this by reducing the number of people in defense and defense-related activities by over 3 million in the last five years. We are, I think, maintaining a pretty adequate defense. There are some areas where I can criticize it, but we've gotten a rather major peace dividend in the last five years. It continues to be a great benefit, not only in terms of taxes, but to our young people because of the volunteer army.

PAUL DUKE, debate moderator: Along the lines of what you are now saying, Senator Brock, isn't it true that many congressmen this year are reluctant to cut the military budget because of the economic slowdown?

SENATOR BROCK: I hear that said, but I don't believe that I have, in the twelve years I've been in Congress, ever heard a member of Congress say, "Well, I'm not going to cut it because we can't afford it in terms of the economy." I think there's a different reason for the support of the defense budget this year—and that's the experience we had last year in the Middle East.

MR. DUKE: You mean the fear of the Russians.

SENATOR BROCK: Well, the Russians—not only with their airlift into that troubled area and the worsening of the conflict because of their involvement, but also because we suddenly became aware of their capability to move in there very fast—their direct overt threat to come in with a significant deployment of troops. There is, I think, a question as to whether we could have stopped them without the use of nuclear weapons; that is something that you just don't want to face. It's a dangerous situation.

DONALD HERZBERG, Georgetown University: Recently a Red Chinese political leader observed that what we are witnessing in the world today is the gradual replacement of U.S. military power around the world with Soviet military power. I wonder if the senators would comment on that.

SENATOR BROCK: Well, they're making quite an effort. For example, they are building their fleet into an offensive weapon for the first time—we haven't seen that before. Russia has always been a land power. The Russians have never been much concerned about their sea power, but they are incredibly strong today. *Jane's Fighting Ships* for the first time in the history of the publication said that as of this past year Russia became the dominant power on the sea.

That's not an encouraging development. They're operating in the Indian Ocean; they now have bases down there which are a threat to the peace of the entire Middle East. That's a matter, I think, of great concern.

SENATOR MUSKIE: Well, I think it's a matter of comparison over time. There's no question that the Soviets have undertaken to expand their influence beyond their borders. They are building a navy to expand their reach over the world's oceans. There's no way that we can eliminate that drive toward influence for whatever purpose the Soviets have in mind. At the same time, we have clearly—primarily as the result of the Vietnam experience—backed off from the interventionist policies that marked our world leadership from World War II until the present. We've decided not to try to police the world. Our people are not willing to continue to support the kind of military presence that we were able to exert around the world at the peak of our posture in the mid-fifties and sixties.

And so the result is that we backed off from our peak effort around the world and the Soviets have expanded. The result is a change in our relative positions. That's why I think it's terribly important that we be very selective in the ways in which we spend our defense dollars.

I'm for maintaining our naval presence. I think we've got to build our navy up above the low point to which it has now fallen, as our World War II ships have become obsolete. I'm interested in such ships as the patrol frigate which is, I think, a low-cost way of building naval presence through small ships. I'm for this and I'm for the submarine deterrent, as I think it is our most nearly invulnerable deterrent at the present time.

And so we have to preserve our place. But if what we long for is the time when we were the dominant power, as we were right after World War II, that would be awfully expensive and I don't think it would serve our national interests.

LESLIE GELB, *New York Times*: I'm trying to think of what you gentlemen have been saying in terms of how it's being heard or will be heard by that famous citizen in Peoria.

And I would guess that in listening to it he would find himself very confused. Here Senator Brock is asserting that we have to worry about Soviet nuclear missiles and Senator Muskie is saying it's not so much of a worry—in fact we're ahead of them.

We have some air force generals saying we have to worry about Soviet tactical air forces and yet we have the chairman of the Joint Chiefs of Staff having said that our tactical air forces can cripple the Soviet tactical air forces. You have the navy saying we have to worry about the Soviet shipbuilding program and a report by the Brookings Institution saying we don't have to worry about it.

How does he make up his mind? Can't we narrow the debate in terms of something that is decidable? You, Senator Brock, said you are in favor of cuts in the defense budget. You can see areas for efficiency. Senator Muskie hinted at those, too. Could you specify what those might be and what they would add up to in savings?

SENATOR BROCK: I'm not sure I'm talking so much about cuts as I am shifts. For example, both of us have supported the Hi-Lo concept. That makes a lot of sense. I suggested at the outset, a phase-in of our strategic programs like Triad; not trying to do them all at the same time.

I suggested that we do more research and development without production. These are things that are specific line items where I think we can effect savings, but I'm not so sure that I really think our research and development is adequate.

Let me just turn it around on you and say that I'm not sure we ought to be debating line items or even dollars. I think we ought to try to decide if there is a price to defense, what is it that we can bear and have some assurance that we're protecting the security of this country.

And, you know, anything else really is almost irrelevant. I can't make a decision between weapons systems. I'm not qualified, and I'm not sure that any of us are.

I can say that whatever it takes, I think the people of my state are willing to pay a price to ensure that their children live in peace—that's the price.

SENATOR MUSKIE: Well, with respect to the specific weapons systems, I would agree with Senator Brock that you can get differences of opinion. But I can suggest some specific weapons systems that I think—

MR. GELB: No, I was talking about efficiency cuts apart from these weapons systems. Again, you can argue back and forth on each one of these weapons systems—

SENATOR MUSKIE: That's right. I'd agree with that.

MR. GELB: —and I was trying to get into something that might be decidable or discernible, where the opinions don't vary as much as you gentlemen have been expressing this evening.

SENATOR BROCK: I do think we would agree on efficiency cuts in a number of areas. It's with the program cuts—it's with the weapon item cuts that we're going to have the problems.

MR. GELB: But what efficiency cuts would you agree on, Senator?

SENATOR BROCK: Well, I thought I listed some in terms of facing—

MR. GELB: You cut in some areas, but you increase R & D and the level remains the same.

SENATOR BROCK: That's correct. So maybe I'm not cutting. Maybe I'm just saying our R & D is not adequate in terms of what's going to happen by 1980.

TED MANN, LTV Aerospace Corporation: I have the same concern as our good friend from the *New York Times* about our people in Peoria. And I have a question for Senator Muskie: so that the man in Peoria can put things in perspective, don't you feel it would be fair not to keep talking about increased budgets when that really ignores the tremendous impact of inflation, which means it's obviously going to go up every year? And shouldn't we really be talking just about the procurement part of the budget, setting aside the entire $50 million that now goes to pay for this wonderful volunteer army? We're really looking at about a $35 billion procurement/hardware budget, and I don't think our friend in Peoria knows that.

SENATOR MUSKIE: Well, my emphasis was different. Fifty-five percent of the budget is manpower. I put a conservative figure of $2 billion on the cuts that I think we could make there without cutting into combat effectiveness at all: cutting into support personnel, cutting into excessive civilian personnel, and cutting into excessive "grade creep" —that is, too high a percentage of officers in relation to enlisted men. Now, just in those categories, you can save at least $2 billion, and there are those who say you can save up to $5 billion in manpower.

That has nothing to do with procurement. However, I do think that you can make cuts in strategic arms along the lines that I've suggested. The secretary of defense's new policy is to begin to develop accuracy and counterforce capability—I think that's destabilizing. I don't think it's necessary for the success of the SALT talks; it doesn't add all that much to this year's budget, but it means billions of dollars down the road.

DISCUSSION

With respect to conventional weapons, there you've got a mix. I think that we're going for some high-cost options that we can stretch out or do without. We should turn our emphasis to low-cost options like the standoff bomber or the smaller submarine, for instance, that would save money down the road.

And so I think in that respect, the procurement budget is a potential source of savings.

SENATOR BROCK: But if I may point out, the inflation alone has eaten up far more than what you're talking about. If you take the cuts that the senator is suggesting, and add them to inflation, we are having a real reduction again in our national defense.

And that leads to a position where, if you continue it very long—and we've been doing it now for five years—you're going to place this nation at some point within the next five to seven years in a position where, as that study showed, we could be subject to a first strike—and I don't think that the people of this country, Peoria or anywhere else, want to be put in that position.

We simply cannot afford to play any games, take any chances with our opportunity to preserve, protect, and defend this country and to maintain a deterrent posture. And that's the basic question. I just don't believe you can accept this kind of cut without placing us in jeopardy.

SENATOR MUSKIE: Senator, only half of the increase is attributed by Secretary Schlesinger himself to inflation in pay increases. The rest of it is attributable to growth in the budget.

MR. DUKE: Unfortunately we have run out of time. Thank you for being with us tonight. [Applause.]

NOTES

NOTES TO FIRST LECTURE

[1] Quoted in Alain C. Enthoven and K. Wayne Smith, *How Much Is Enough? Shaping the Defense Program, 1961-1969* (New York: Harper & Row, 1971), p. 35.

[2] "Report from the Council of Economic Advisers—Message from the President," *Congressional Record* (28 May 1974), p. S. 8950.

[3] U.S. Congress, Senate, Committee on Armed Services, *Hearings on S.3000*, 93rd Congress, 2nd session (5 February 1974), p. 26.

[4] Ibid.

NOTES TO SECOND LECTURE

[1] General Maxwell D. Taylor, "The Legitimate Claims of National Security," *Foreign Affairs*, vol. 52, no. 3 (April 1974), p. 592.

[2] *Commanders' Digest*, vol. 15, no. 16 (18 April 1974), p. 12.

[3] *Military Policy and Budget Priorities: Fiscal Year 1975* (Washington, D. C.: Project on Budget Priorities, 1974).

[4] *Studying National Priorities: The 1974 Budget* (Washington, D. C.: The Brookings Institution, 1973), p. 403.

[5] Secretary of State Kissinger's news conference of 3 January 1974, reported in the *Department of State Bulletin*, vol. 70, no. 1805 (28 January 1974), p. 85.

[6] "Legitimate Claims of National Security," p. 577.

NOTE TO REBUTTALS

[1] Barry M. Blechman, et al., *Setting National Priorities: The 1975 Budget* (Washington, D. C.: The Brookings Institution, 1974), p. 112.